Collins · FLAGSHIP HISTORYMAKERS

Series Editor: Derrick Murphy

LENIN

Collins · FLAGSHIP HISTORYMAKERS

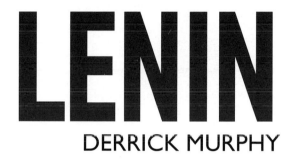

DERRICK MURPHY

An imprint of HarperCollins*Publishers*

William Collins' dream of knowledge for all began
with the publication of his first book in 1819. A self-
educated mill worker, he not only enriched millions
of lives, but also founded a flourishing publishing
house. Today, staying true to this spirit, Collins
books are packed with inspiration, innovation and
practical expertise. They place you at the centre of a
world of possibility and give you exactly what you
need to explore it.

Collins. Do more.

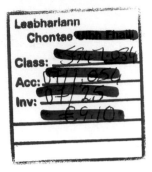
Published by Collins
An imprint of HarperCollins*Publishers*
77–85 Fulham Palace Road
Hammersmith
London
W6 8JB

You might also like to visit
www.harpercollins.co.uk
The book lovers' website

Browse the complete Collins catalogue at
www.collinseducation.com

© HarperCollins*Publishers* Ltd 2005

10 9 8 7 6 5 4 3 2 1

ISBN 0 00 719916 3

British Library Cataloguing in Publication Data
A Catalogue record for this publication is available
from the British Library

Series commissioned by Graham Bradbury
Project management by Marie Insall
Edited by Claire Andrews
Book design by Derek Lee
Map artwork by Richard Morris
Picture research by Celia Dearing
Production by Sarah Robinson
Printed and bound by Printing Express, Hong Kong

Contents

Why do historians differ?

THE purpose of the Flagship Historymakers series is to explore the main debates surrounding a number of key individuals in British, European and American History.

Each book begins with a chronology of the significant events in the life of the particular individual, and an outline of the person's career. The book then examines in greater detail three of the most important and controversial issues in the life of the individual – issues which continue to attract differing views from historians, and which feature prominently in examination syllabuses in A-level History and beyond.

Each of these issue sections provides students with an overview of the main argument put forward by historians. By posing key questions, these sections aim to help students to think through the areas of debate and to form their own judgments on the evidence. It is important, therefore, for students to understand why historians differ in their views on past events and, in particular, on the role of individuals in past events.

The study of history is an ongoing debate about events in the past. Although factual evidence is the essential ingredient of history, it is the *interpretation* of factual evidence that forms the basis for historical debate. The study of why historians differ is termed 'historiography'.

Historical debate can occur for a wide variety of reasons.

Insufficient evidence

In some cases there is insufficient evidence to provide a definitive conclusion. In attempting to 'fill the gaps' where factual evidence is unavailable, historians use their professional judgements to make 'informed comments' about the past.

New evidence

As new evidence comes to light, an historian today may have more information on which to base judgements than historians in the past. With any study of Lenin, official records are problematic. Before the collapse of communism in Russia it was the Soviet authorities who determined who could study archival material. As a result, western historians had to rely on the views of exiles and any information which the Soviet authorities decided to release. Since the fall of the USSR in 1991, historians have been given much greater access to Russian archives.

'A philosophy of history?'

Many historians have a specific view of history that will affect the way they make their historical judgements. For instance, Marxist historians – who take the view from the writings of Karl Marx the founder of modern socialism – believe that society has always been made up of competing economic and social classes. They also place considerable importance on economic reasons in human decision making. Therefore, a Marxist historian looking at an historical issue may take a completely different viewpoint to a non-Marxist historian. To Marxist historians the collapse of the Tsarist regime was an historical inevitability. However, even amongst Marxists, Lenin's decision to push for a Bolshevik-led revolution so shortly after the creation of a liberal republic has caused some controversy.

The role of the individual

Some historians have seen past history as being largely moulded by the acts of specific individuals. Lenin, Hitler and Stalin are seen as individuals whose personality and beliefs changed the course of twentieth-century history. Other historians have tended to play down the role of individuals; instead, they highlight the importance of more general social, economic and political change. Rather than seeing Lenin as an individual who changed the course of political history, these historians tend to see him as representing the views of the Russian working class and peasantry at that time. A socialist revolution would have taken place with or without Lenin.

Placing different emphasis on the same historical evidence

Even if historians do not possess different philosophies of history or place different emphasis on the role of the individual, it is still possible for them to disagree in one very important way. This is that they may place different emphases on aspects of the same factual evidence. As a result, History should be seen as a subject that encourages debate about the past, based on historical evidence.

Summary

Historical debate is, in its nature, continuous. What today may be an accepted view about a past event may well change in the future, as the debate continues.

Timeline: Lenin's life

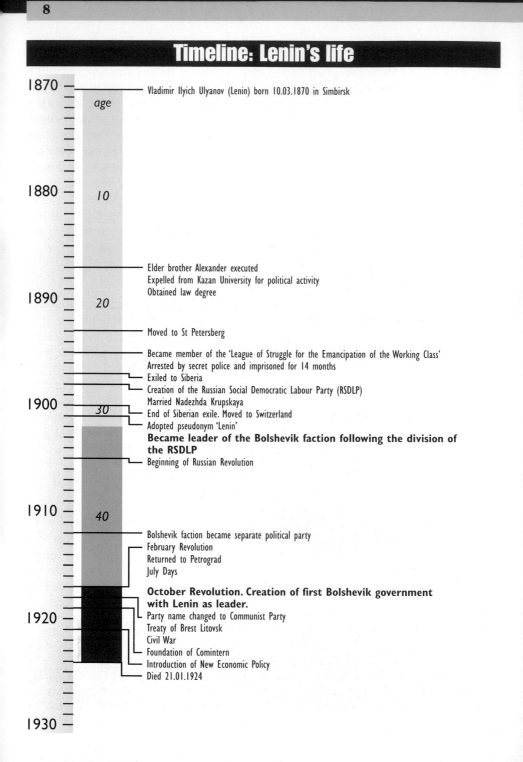

1870 — Vladimir Ilyich Ulyanov (Lenin) born 10.03.1870 in Simbirsk

age

1880 — 10

Elder brother Alexander executed
Expelled from Kazan University for political activity
Obtained law degree

1890 — 20

Moved to St Petersberg

Became member of the 'League of Struggle for the Emancipation of the Working Class'
Arrested by secret police and imprisoned for 14 months
Exiled to Siberia
Creation of the Russian Social Democratic Labour Party (RSDLP)
Married Nadezhda Krupskaya

1900 — 30
End of Siberian exile. Moved to Switzerland
Adopted pseudonym 'Lenin'

Became leader of the Bolshevik faction following the division of the RSDLP
Beginning of Russian Revolution

1910 — 40

Bolshevik faction became separate political party
February Revolution
Returned to Petrograd
July Days

October Revolution. Creation of first Bolshevik government with Lenin as leader.
Party name changed to Communist Party
Treaty of Brest Litovsk

1920 —
Civil War
Foundation of Comintern
Introduction of New Economic Policy
Died 21.01.1924

1930 —

Lenin addressing the crowd around the time of the October Revolution, 1917

Lenin: a brief biography

How did he make history?

Revolutionary: a person who supports drastic ideas which oppose those of a political system or society.

Bolshevik Party: one of the emergent factions of the split of the RSDLP caused by polarised views concerning party organisation and revolutionary violence. The Bolsheviks supported the political system introduced by Lenin after the Russian Revolution in 1917.

October Revolution (1917): the armed takeover of the Provisional Government by the Bolsheviks led by Lenin in 1917.

Communism: a political movement based on the writings of Marx, which advocates a classless society based on public ownership of the means of production. Lenin renamed his Bolshevik Party the Communist Party in 1918.

Soviet Union: the Union of Soviet Socialist Republics (USSR) was established in 1922 as a Communist state and lasted until the end of the Cold War in 1991. It was the largest country in the world, occupying a seventh of the total land surface.

Dictatorship: government by a dictator who holds supreme power or authority.

Lenin (1870–1924) was a major political philosopher, a professional **revolutionary** and, from 1917, a leading Russian statesman. It was Lenin's determination that led to the formation of the **Bolshevik Party**, which seized power in Russia in the **October Revolution**, creating the world's first **Communist** state. By the time of Lenin's death in January 1924 the **Soviet Union (USSR)** had been established.

Yet the 'cult of personality' surrounding him has meant that Lenin's place in history has transcended even his death. Lenin has been credited with devising a way of turning **Karl Marx**'s views on society into reality. His Bolshevik/Communist Party has provided a model for socialist revolutionaries all over the globe and Marxist-Leninism has become the political basis for the international growth of communism. By the late 1980s, over one third of the world's population lived under communist rule in states within Europe, Asia and Latin America, all of which looked back to Lenin as their inspiration.

However, since the collapse of communist rule in eastern Europe and the end of the Soviet Union, views on Lenin have changed dramatically; many have blamed him for setting up the system of political repression and **dictatorship** that has become associated with communist rule. So who or what was the real Lenin?

Family background

Lenin was born Vladimir Ilyich Ulyanov on 10 March 1870 in the provincial Russian town of Simbirsk on the River Volga. He was born into a wealthy family; his father, Ilya, was a provincial school inspector, a position equivalent to that of a member of the Russian nobility.

Vladmir (Russian for 'rule the world') was a quiet, studious boy, who excelled at Latin, Greek, History, Geography and Russian literature. His headmaster, K.M. Kerensky, was the father of

Karl Marx (1818–83)
A German political philosopher and founding father of Marxism (Communism). Marx believed that history was a series of class struggles which would inevitably lead to the triumph of the proletariat (working class).

**Tsar Alexander III
(1845–94)**
Became Tsar in 1881
following the assassination of
his father, Alexander II.
Ruthlessly repressed political
reformers and those who
were not members of the
Russian Orthodox Church,
and pursued a policy of
'Russification' — imposing the
Russian language and schools
upon national minorities
living in the Russian Empire.
Died in 1894 and was
succeeded by his son,
Nicholas II.

Alexander Kerensky, who was later to be leader of the Provisional Government that was overthrown by Lenin in October 1917.

In 1887 Vladimir's brother, Alexander, was arrested and executed for his involvement in a plot to assassinate **Tsar Alexander III**. Alexander's death, which closely followed that of his father, meant that, within two years, Vladimir became the head of the family at the age of 17.

The making of a revolutionary

The impact that Alexander's death had on his brother is clear in an eight-line autobiography, written in April 1917:

> 'My name is Vladimir Ilyich Ulyanov. I was born in Simbirsk on 10th April 1870. In the spring of 1887, my older brother Alexander was executed by Alexander III for an attempt (March 1st 1887) on his life.'

Indeed, there is no evidence to suggest that Vladimir held any revolutionary views before this time, but from 1887 he became actively involved in revolutionary affairs. He was arrested in December 1895 for being a member of an illegal revolutionary organisation. After spending 14 months in prison, Vladimir was exiled to Siberia for three years, where he received a monthly allowance of eight roubles from the government, and had the freedom to visit the local town of Shushenskoe. He read and wrote extensively during this time, but perhaps the most important event of Vladimir's period of exile was his marriage to Nazedhka Krupskaya, who he had met in St Petersburg prior to his arrest. Their marriage, although childless, was to last until his death in 1924.

As a revolutionary, Vladimir wrote under several assumed names including 'Frei', 'Ilyin', 'Tulin' and 'Jacob Richter'. By 1901 he had settled on 'Lenin', which is generally accepted as meaning 'man from the Lena River', a large river in Siberia.

In 1902, after fleeing to Switzerland, Lenin wrote *What is to be Done?* in which he set out his plan to create a political party of professional revolutionaries to overthrow the Tsar. This idea led to a split with other Russian Marxists at the Second Congress of the **RSDLP** in London in 1903. Lenin's supporters were known as the Bolshevik faction within the RSDLP; they eventually broke away in 1912 to form their own political party.

By 1917 Lenin was committed to a more violent means of

RSDLP: the Russian Social Democratic Party, which was founded in 1898. From 1903 to 1912 the RSDLP contained a number of factions including the Bolsheviks, the Mensehviks, the Inter-District Group and the Jewish Bund.

Petrograd: formerly St Petersburg, Russia's capital until 1918, which was renamed in the patriotic spirit associated with the outbreak of the First World War. Became Leningrad in honour of Lenin after his death in 1924. Reverted to St Petersburg in the early 1990s, following the collapse of the USSR.

Provisional Government: temporary government set up by former members of Tsar Nicholas II's parliament after his abdication.

***April Theses* (1917)**: Lenin's ten-point programme outlining the continuation of the revolution against the Provisional Government.

All Russia Soviet: one of the worker's councils which emerged during the failed Revolution of 1905 and rivalled the Provisional Government.

Kornilov Affair: events of late August 1917 when the commander-in-chief of the Russian Army, Lavr Kornilov, planned to send troops to Petrograd to thwart what he thought was a Bolshevik uprising. The head of the Provisional Government, Alexander Kerensky, misinterpreted Kornilov's actions as a attempted military coup. Kerensky armed the Petrograd workers and arrested Kornilov. The Affair caused widespread fear of a right-wing uprising.

Coup d'etat: a sudden violent or illegal overthrow of government, usually by a small group.

bringing down the Russian political system, aiming to replace it with a state dominated by the Russian industrial working class.

The rise to power 1917

When the Tsar was finally deposed in February 1917, Lenin was in Zurich, but he was able to return to Russia with the assistance of the German government. When Lenin returned to **Petrograd** in April 1917 he caused a sensation. Instead of supporting the **Provisional Government** that had replaced the Tsar, he called for its overthrow. In his ***April Theses*** Lenin put forward a plan for the Bolsheviks to take power, and in June and July the Bolsheviks held demonstrations in the hope of achieving this end. These attempts failed, however, and Lenin fled to Finland, where he remained until October that year.

One of the tactics Lenin used to achieve his aim of destroying the Provisional Government was his proclamation of 'All Power to the Soviets'. The **All Russia Soviet** was an assembly of workers, peasants and soldiers that provided a rival source of power to the Provisional Government. Lenin also demanded 'Peace, Bread and Land': an end to the war, food for the cities and land to the peasants. Both appeals proved popular and Bolshevik support increased from July to October. A further aid to the Bolshevik cause was the **Kornilov Affair** of August 1917, when the head of the army, **Lavr Kornilov**, was accused of trying to create a military dictatorship. When Kornilov failed, fear of a right-wing coup meant that support for the Bolsheviks greatly increased.

Lenin called for the Bolsheviks to use armed means to seize power before the Second All Russia Congress of Soviets met at the end of October, as he wanted to use a Bolshevik majority at the Congress to give support to a Bolshevik **coup d'etat.**

On 24 and 25 October, armed units arrested members of the Provisional Government and replaced them with Bolsheviks. Within the space of seven months, Lenin had risen from being the leader of a party of Russian socialists to the head of government.

Lavr Kornilov (1870–1918)
An imperial Russian army general best known for the Kornilov Affair of 1917.

Kornilov was arrested but escaped and later became one of the commanders of the White Army during the Civil War.

Understanding Lenin

■ Rebelling against his wealthy background, Lenin spent his adult life attempting to destroy Russian middle-class society.

■ A committed Marxist who believed in the rule of the proletariat.

■ Described as looking like a 'provincial grocer', Lenin was short, prematurely bald at the age of 20, and wore a cloth cap.

■ A revolutionary who advocated the violent seizure of power.

■ A dictator who created a repressive regime based on political terror.

■ A disruptive, divisive force who sought ultimate power at the expense of socialist unity.

■ Intolerant of alternative views and uncompromising, Lenin demanded total subservience from Party members.

■ A forceful personality, Lenin possessed a charismatic presence when speaking. His rhetorical skills were powerful enough to win over potential challengers.

■ Treated politics like warfare – his opponents, both internal and external, had to be crushed by whatever means necessary.

■ Personally a coward who ran at the first sign of trouble and never once visited his troops in action during the Civil War.

■ An opportunist to whom the end justified the means, Lenin continually revised his policies to take advantage of changing circumstances.

■ During and after his lifetime a 'cult of personality' developed, praising Lenin as an almost god-like figure in Russian history.

> *'His strength of will, indomitable discipline, energy, and unshakeable faith in the cause had an effect that can only be conveyed by the overused word "charisma".'*
> Richard Pipes

Ruler of Russia 1917–24

Winning power was relatively easy in October 1917 as the Provisional Government had lost virtually all support, but keeping power was another matter. In November there were elections to a Constituent Assembly, which would decide the future government of Russia. The Bolsheviks achieved 25 per cent of the vote but the largest party were the **Social Revolutionaries (SRs)** with 40 per cent of the vote.

Social Revolutionaries (SRs): a radical group who wanted land to be transferred to the Russian peasantry.

Lenin used a variety of means to maintain power. Between December 1917 and March 1918 he formed a coalition government with the Left SRs. In addition, he launched a campaign of political terror against his opponents using the **Cheka**. His most notable strategy, however, was the dissolution of the Constituent Assembly in January 1918.

Cheka: the first Soviet state security organisation set up to tackle counter-revolutionaries and foreign enemies.

The most serious problem faced by Lenin was the **Civil War** of 1918–20. Faced with **White forces** who opposed Bolshevik rule, the survival of Lenin's government was dependent on the Whites' ineffective organisation and the effective leadership of the **Red Army**.

Civil War (1918–20): an attempted counter-revolution by the Whites: a loose coalition of opponents including landowners, those who wanted a return to a democracy and some socialists and former WWI allies. The Bolsheviks, known as the Reds, defeated them.

During the Civil War Lenin introduced War Communism, a policy that nationalised all industry and also forcibly took food from the peasants. It proved to be disastrous. The war took a terrible toll on Russia, over six million died – many from the famine of 1921/2 – and industry was all but destroyed. Cities shrank in size as people fled to the countryside looking for food.

White forces: the Russian political and military forces that opposed the Bolsheviks after the October Revolution.

In March 1921 the Soviet state was at crisis point. At Kronstadt, sailors of the Baltic Fleet rose up in rebellion against communist repression. At the Tenth Party Congress Lenin proposed a New Economic Policy, which gave greater freedom to the peasants.

Red Army: the name of the Bolshevik army set up by Leon Trotsky in 1918.

Lenin's greatest failure after October 1917 was his attempt to spread communism outside the old Russian Empire. In 1919 he created an international organisation for that purpose, **Comintern**. Uprisings took place in Germany and Hungary but all attempts to create other communist governments failed. In 1920 Lenin supported a war against Poland to spread communism but Russia was badly defeated.

Comintern: the Third Communist International set up in 1919 to coordinate the activities of communist parties worldwide.

By the time of his death, Lenin had started a great political revolution within Russia and created the Soviet Union. Yet he had not achieved true communism but rather an uneasy alliance of the Communist Party, workers and peasants. It would take Lenin's successor, Stalin, to complete the social and economic revolution that Lenin had begun.

1

Did Lenin help or hinder the development of Russian socialism in the years 1895–1917?

How far did he adapt Marx's ideas to Russian conditions?

Was he merely an opportunist?

How successful was he in controlling the Bolsheviks from 1903 to 1917?

Was he a help or hindrance to Russian socialism?

Framework of events

1895	Lenin visited the leading Russian Marxists, Plekhanov and Axelrod, in Switzerland
	Lenin exiled in Siberia
1900	RSDLP founded
	Lenin moved to Switzerland
	Lenin founded *Iskra*
1902	Publication of *What is to be Done?*
1903	Second Party Congress of RSDLP. Split into Bolshevik and Menshevik factions
1905	Revolution in Russia
	Lenin returned to Russia in November
1906	First Duma
	Lenin went to Finland
1907	Lenin lived in Geneva, Switzerland
1912	Bolshevik Party formed. *Pravda* published as party newspaper
1914	Outbreak of First World War
1915	Prague Congress. Lenin supported idea of civil war between workers and their national governments
	Imperialism, the Highest Stage of Capitalism published
1917	February Revolution. Tsar overthrown and replaced by Provisional Government
	Lenin returned to Russia aided by German government
	April Theses published
	October Revolution: Bolsheviks seized political power in Russia

Mikhail Gorbachev (born 1931)
President of the Soviet Union from 1985 to 1991. His reforms led to the end of the Cold War but also unintentionally brought to an end the supremacy of his Communist Party and caused the break up of the Soviet Union.

Ideology: a set of ideas.

L ENIN'S role in the development of socialism is considered to be the defining feature of his career. Lenin's ideas remained virtually unquestioned during the entire period of communist rule in Russia (1917–91). Even during the period of *glasnost* (openness) and *perestroika* (restructuring) under **Gorbachev** (1985–1991), Lenin's views were held up as an example of how the USSR could rediscover its position as a global superpower. Yet was Lenin's contribution to the development of socialism always clear and helpful?

The standard Soviet view was that Lenin was the natural successor to Karl Marx, as it was he who had first put Marx's ideas into practice. Eventually Lenin's ideas brought about the establishment of the first communist state and became the foundation for the international development of communism. When Mao Zedong created the People's Republic of China in 1949, and when, ten year's later, Fidel Castro established his rule in Cuba, it was Marx and Lenin from whom they both drew inspiration. Marxist-Leninism became the political **ideology** on which communist regimes throughout the world were based.

How far did Lenin adapt Marx's ideas to Russian conditions?

Socialism: an economic system in which the means of production, distribution and exchange are owned by the community collectively, usually through the state. A more moderate version of communism, which aims to create a society where political, social and economic power are equally distributed among the population.

Capitalism: the social and economic system created by industrialisation, which involves the private ownership of industry and business and is characterised by profit and competition.

What were Marx's main ideas?

It was in the mid-nineteenth century that Karl Marx (1818–83) began to develop his form of socialism, which became known as Marxism. Marx's principal socialist ideas were contained in *The Communist Manifesto* (1848) and *Das Kapital* (Capital) (1867).

For Marx, **socialism** was the solution to the social, economic and political problems created by **capitalism**. Marx believed that as capitalism developed, economic power would be concentrated in fewer and fewer hands and, as a result, the majority of the population would become less and less wealthy.

Marx's views on history were based on the idea of class struggle. An earlier feudal system had been replaced by a capitalist society associated with industrialisation, where there was conflict between factory owners and businessmen – the 'bourgeoisie' – and the industrial working class, or 'proletariat'. The final development of society would take place when the industrial working class eventually overthrew capitalism to create a socialist society within which social equality would prevail.

Marxists believed that, as Russia had been a feudal society until 1917, before socialism could be achieved there would have to be a capitalist phase where the bourgeoisie were the dominant class. However, for Lenin and other Russian Marxists, the timescale between a capitalist/bourgeois revolution and a proletarian/socialist revolution was a matter of intense debate.

What was Russian society like at the end of the nineteenth century?

The Russian Empire was the largest country on earth, covering 20 per cent of the world's land surface. Russia was an 'autocracy': all political power was held by the Tsar, or Emperor of Russia. **Nicholas II** was Tsar from 1894 until his murder by the Bolsheviks in 1918.

From 1864 a limited form of elected local government (*zemstvo*) was allowed, which controlled matters such as local education and road maintenance.

In October 1905, at the height of the Russian Revolution, the Tsar changed the Russian constitution, creating a nationally-elected parliament – the State Duma. The Duma had very limited powers, however, as the government remained under the Tsar's control. Moreover, not all Russians were allowed to vote for the Duma; from 1907 the electoral law was so narrow that only the relatively wealthy could vote. It was not until after 1905 that some political parties became tolerated by the Tsar's government.

**Tsar Nicholas II
(1894–1917)**
The last Tsar of the Romanov dynasty that had ruled the Russian Empire from 1613. The Tsars ruled as autocrats (monarchs with absolute power) and Nicholas's reign was epitomised by force and repression. He and his family were executed by the communists in 1918 during the Russian Civil War (1918–20).

The idea of socialist ideas being popular in late nineteenth-century Russia might seem peculiar as, of all the major powers of Europe, Russia was the most economically backward. Eighty per cent of the population were peasants who worked in agriculture and rented land from landowners or the Tsar. Industry only existed on a small scale in cities such as St Petersburg and Moscow and in the coalfields of the eastern Ukraine.

Lenin's socialist development

Lenin's development as a revolutionary can be seen to pre-date his interest in socialism and the writings of Karl Marx. His opposition to the autocratic rule of the Tsars dates from 1887, when his elder brother, Alexander, was tried and executed for having been part of a plot to assassinate Tsar Alexander III. Lenin became a follower of

Marx in 1888/9 after reading *Das Kapital*. He was expelled from Kazan University for political activity in 1889 and joined the Russian Marxist movement in 1892/3. In December 1895 Vladimir was arrested by the Okhrana (Tsarist secret police) and imprisoned for 14 months for his role in an illegal revolutionary organisation called 'The League of Struggle for the Emancipation of the Working Class' and was later exiled to Siberia for three years.

As a Marxist, Lenin was in a minority among Russian revolutionaries. Until the 1890s the most popular revolutionary group was the Populists, who believed that political and economic power should be handed over to the Russian peasantry. One extremist Populist group, the 'People's Will', had been responsible for the assassination of Tsar Alexander II in 1881 and other terrorist attacks on government officials. Populism enjoyed favour in Russia well into the twentieth century.

In 1900 the Socialist Revolutionary party was formed. This was the direct descendent of Populism. The Socialist Revolutionaries (SRs) supported peasant ownership of land and remained the largest revolutionary party until the creation of the communist dictatorship in 1917.

As a new member of the Russian Marxist movement, Lenin looked towards **Georgi Plekhanov** and **Pavel Axelrod**, the leading Russian Marxists of the 1890s, who were both living in exile in Switzerland. Exile was also to be Lenin's fate from much of the period up to April 1917. He spent three years in internal exile in Siberia from 1897 to 1900, and was then exiled abroad until 1917, except for a short period during the 1905 Russian Revolution.

Georgi Plekhanov (1856–1918)

A leading Russian revolutionary and Marxist theoretician, who set up the 'League of Struggle for the Emancipation of the Working Class' of which Lenin was a member. Also founder of the SR movement. Plekhanov sided with the Mensheviks when the RSDLP split in 1903 and was hostile towards the Bolshevik revolution.

Pavel Axelrod (1850–1928)

A leading socialist who became a Menshevik when the RSDLP split. Co-editor of *Iskra*. Axelrod called the October Revolution a 'historical crime without parallel in modern history' and toured the world rallying socialist opposition to the Bolsheviks.

Political groups and parties in Russia 1895–1917

The Russian Social Democratic Labour Party (RSDLP) or Social Democrats

Marxists who aimed to overthrow the Tsar and establish a socialist society.

At the Second Party Congress in London in 1903 the party split into two major factions: the Bolsheviks who supported Lenin, and the Mensheviks led by Yuli Martov. (There were other groups such as the Jewish Bund and the Inter-District Group).

■ Bolsheviks: (known as Communists from 1918). Lenin's party.

■ Mensheviks: Members of the RSDLP who supported the Provisional Government and wanted to see the establishment of a liberal democratic republic before a socialist revolution took place.

Socialist Revolutionaries (SRs)

This radical group wanted to redistribute all land to the Russian peasantry. Unsurprisingly, as peasants comprised 80 per cent of the population, it became the most widely supported party in Russia.

The Party was always a local grouping and, in August 1917, a radical group split from the party to become the Left SRs. They later formed a brief coalition government with the Bolsheviks in 1917–18.

The Liberals

Members of the middle class who wanted more political freedom in Russia. From 1905 they were divided into two main groups:

■ Octobrists, who regarded the 1905 October Manifesto as the basis for the Russian political system and the limit for constitutional change.

■ Constitutional Democrats (Kadets), who saw the October Manifesto as the first step towards full parliamentary government for Russia.

The Conservatives (Tsarists)

This political group aimed to preserve the Tsarist government.

Lenin (centre) and Yuli Martov (seated right) were both members of the League of Struggle for the Emancipation of the Working Class, 1897.

What was Lenin's contribution to the development of Russian socialism?

Lenin's contribution to both the development of socialist ideas for Russia and the international Marxist movement was immense. His first major work, *The Economic Development of Russia* was published in 1899. Its significance lies in Lenin's classification of Russian peasants as poor, middle or rich. Lenin was later to develop the idea that a class struggle existed in the Russian countryside between poor peasants and *kulaks* (rich peasants) and wrote of an alliance of industrial workers and poor peasants working together to create a socialist revolutionary state.

Lenin's greatest contribution to the development of Russian socialism was the creation of a disciplined faction dedicated to revolution. Such a group was set up at around the time of the RSDLP split in 1903, shortly after the publication of Lenin's pamphlet, *What is to be Done?* in which he cited the need for a group of professional revolutionaries to bring about revolutionary change on behalf of the industrial workers and poor peasants. In his words: 'give us an organisation of revolutionaries and we shall turn Russia upside down'.

The emergence of the Bolshevik faction

The first major conflict within the RSDLP arose during the Second Party Congress. Lenin wanted membership to be limited to those who were actively involved in implementing the party programme. **Yuli Martov**, on the other hand, wanted membership broadened to include all those who accepted the party programme. Despite an initial defeat by 28 votes to 22, when the **Jewish Bund** left the Congress Lenin was able to get his view accepted by 17 votes to 15. This led to a split in the RSDLP; those who supported Lenin became known as Bolsheviks (the majority) and those who supported Yuli Martov, Mensheviks (the minority); in reality the Mensheviks always outnumbered the Bolsheviks in membership.

In Prague in January 1912 Lenin called a special conference at which the Bolsheviks declared themselves a separate political party. Following Lenin's seizure of power in 1918 the Bolshevik Party was renamed the Communist Party and, from that time on, their party structure became the model for communist parties all over the world. In 1919 the Third Communist International (Comintern) of communist parties was created, an organisation that owed its leadership, direction and inspiration to Lenin.

Yuli Martov (1873–1923)
Born Yuly Isederbaum. Originally a member of the Jewish Bund of socialists, he was a close friend of Lenin and was on the editorial board of *Iskra*. In 1903 Martov split with Lenin over the definition of membership of the RSDLP and became leader of the Menshevik faction.

Jewish Bund: The General Jewish Labour Union — a Jewish political party that sought the establishment of a democratic socialist Russia within which Jews would receive legal recognition and anti-semitism would be abolished.

Lenin's version of Marxism

Lenin adapted Marx's ideas to fit Russian conditions. According to Marx, socialism would first occur in the most advanced industrialised countries such as Britain and Germany. In 1916 Lenin wrote the pamphlet *Imperialism, The Highest Stage of Capitalism*, which contradicted Marx, arguing that a socialist revolution could occur in the weakest, not the strongest, part of the capitalist economic system – this was Russia. Lenin believed that revolution could begin in Russia and then spread to advanced industrialised countries.

Upon return from political exile in 1917 Lenin published his *April Theses* in which he claimed that the capitalist phase of revolution could be followed almost immediately by the socialist phase. This shocked virtually all Bolshevik leaders in Russia, who supported Marx's belief that there needed to be a period of time between a capitalist and a socialist revolution. Consequently, one of Lenin's greatest triumphs was persuading the Bolsheviks in Russia to accept his timetable for revolution. The Bolsheviks became the only major political group in Russia to advocate the overthrow of the Provisional Government that had replaced the Tsar's government following the **February Revolution** of 1917.

February Revolution (1917): this involved the abdication of Tsar Nicholas II and the end of the Romanov dynasty. The Tsar was replaced by the Provisional Government.

A Communist poster of Lenin and Marx, bearing the inscription 'Fidelity to Marxism-Leninism is a basis of great victories'.

It could be argued that only a disciplined, centralised party, willing to use a variety of means to seize power, was likely to succeed in the political conditions facing Russia from 1903 to 1917. If that is true, then Lenin did indeed successfully adapt Marx's views to fit Russian conditions.

Lenin's major writings

What is to be Done? (1902)

Advocated the creation of a disciplined party of professional revolutionaries to lead the socialist revolution in Russia. Its title was taken from a novel by the Populist writer N. G. Chernyshevsky in which the leading character, Rakhmetov, is a professional revolutionary.

Imperialism, The Highest Stage of Capitalism (1916)

Lenin's contribution to the Marxist explanation of the outbreak of the First World War. Lenin believed capitalism had led to the creation of large monopolies or cartels that would force their government to resort to war in order to gain more economic power. Lenin also believed that a socialist revolution would break out in the weakest, not the strongest, capitalist economies. He had Russia in mind as 'capitalism's weakest link'.

The April Theses (1917)

Based on five 'Letters from Afar' that Lenin wrote to the Russian Bolsheviks in 1917. Lenin completely redefined Marx's view on history, suggesting that a capitalist-democratic and a social revolution could take place within months of each other. He condemned the Provisional Government and demanded a new socialist revolution.

State and Revolution (1917)

Written following the July Days of 1917, when Lenin had fled to Finland and believed his chance of gaining power had been lost. Lenin supported the idea of a decentralised 'commune' state and this work shows strong evidence of what Lenin attempted to introduce during the early months of his regime in 1917–18.

How successful was Lenin in controlling the Bolsheviks from 1903 to 1917?

The popular image of Lenin presented by Soviet histories is one of total control over his followers. An example of this is *A Short History of the Communist Party of the Soviet Union* (1970), which portrays Lenin as a god-like leader who led the Bolsheviks to victory through his sheer force of character. Such a view is also advocated by many other writers, including the English Marxist historian, Christopher Hill. In the postscript to his work, *Lenin and the Russian Revolution* (1970), Hill refers to Lenin's 'purposefulness, realism, common sense, willpower and pugnacity' in achieving his ends.

Lenin's desire for total control

Alexander Bogdanov (1873–1928)
A physician, scientist, economist, novelist and Marxist philosopher. Bogdanov was a Menshevik whose moderate ideas Lenin relentlessly attacked. After strong disagreements over Marxist theory, proletarian culture, and the means of achieving a socialist revolution, Lenin ousted Bogdanov from the Party.

Lenin did not find controlling the Bolsheviks an easy task. This was due, in part, to Lenin's own personality. Virtually all Lenin's biographers refer to his inability to tolerate alternative views. Even Christopher Hill regards Lenin as secretive and rude towards his colleagues. Lenin was particularly vindictive towards anyone who posed a potential threat to his leadership. This was true of his relationship with **Alexander Bogdanov** between 1904 and 1909. Lenin had become an admirer of Bogdanov as a fund-raiser and Marxist thinker; however, when Bogdanov attempted to set up educational institutions in Russia to teach the workers Marxist ideas, Lenin saw this as a threat to his organisational control and, in 1909, had Bogdanov expelled from the Bolshevik faction.

In *Lenin: the Practice and Theory of Revolution* (2001), the historian James D. White reinforces the idea that Lenin was his own worst enemy in trying to control the Bolsheviks:

'Lenin did not set out to create the Bolshevik Party. He was intent on gaining control over the entire RSDLP. He spent over a decade forming alliances, which he hoped would make this possible. In the end he failed.'

Tactics and propaganda

Following the Second Party Congress, Lenin hoped to control the Bolsheviks in Russia through a network of agents linked to his newspaper *Iskra* (The Spark). By 1904 he had lost control of *Iskra* to the Mensheviks and, in retaliation, created *Vpered* (Forward) as an alternative channel for his views. Finally, when the Bolsheviks declared themselves a separate party in 1912, Lenin launched the party newspaper, *Pravda* (Truth). The growth of *Pravda* was aided by Roman Malinovsky, a Bolshevik leader in the Duma and Lenin's deputy in Russia. Malinovsky was also an agent of the Tsarist secret police, which allowed Pravda a degree of police protection.

Several other of Lenin's tactics were also unpopular with the Bolsheviks, including what were called 'expropriations', essentially bank robberies to raise funds for the party. In fact, so great was opposition to Lenin that in 1910 he lost control of Bolshevik party funds when the Central Committee of the Social Democrats called for conciliation between Bolsheviks and Mensheviks.

The limitations of exile

Another factor that added to Lenin's difficulties in controlling the Bolsheviks was that, apart from a brief return to Russia during the 1905 Revolution, from 1900 Lenin had lived most of his life in exile abroad. Living overseas, Lenin found contact with Russian-based Bolsheviks exceedingly difficult and, as part of an illegal organisation that was constantly harassed by the Tsarist secret police, it was inevitable that Lenin's control and influence were severely limited. According to Richard Pipes in *The Russian Revolution, 1899–1919* (1990), in 1905 the Bolsheviks had approximately 8400 followers, roughly the same as the Mensheviks and the Jewish Bund. At the Stockholm Congress of 1906 Bolshevik numbers had risen to 13 000, compared to 18 000 Mensheviks. In 1907, the RSDLP had grown to 84 300 members, comprising 461 000 Bolsheviks and 38 200 Mensheviks. But by 1910, as a result of repression, numbers for the whole Social Democrat Party had fallen below 10 000.

Lenin overcomes internal opposition

Many Bolsheviks did not accept Lenin's ideological leadership, and there was some resistance to the extremist nature of his ideas. Also, following the split of 1903, many Bolsheviks and Mensheviks attempted reconciliation. Nevertheless, Lenin remained the leader of the Bolsheviks until his death in 1924. No one could match his intellect and determination or his ability to argue his case. His most noticeable triumph in this regard was the conversion of the party to his views following the *April Theses* of 1917; going over the heads of the Bolshevik leadership, Lenin made a direct appeal to the rank and file of the party. Again in September 1917 he was able to persuade the

**Lev Kamenev
(1883–1936)**

Leading Bolshevik who was in exile with Lenin from 1907 to 1914. Opposed the 1917 October Revolution to the point where he publicised his opposition in the press, but later became Lenin's deputy in the Bolshevik government and was also head of the Moscow Soviet and Commissar for Foreign Trade.

**Gregori Zinoviev
(1883–1936)**

Joined Bolsheviks after the 1903 split from the RSDLP. Was in exile with Lenin until 1917. Openly opposed the October rising and later resigned from the Bolshevik government because Lenin refused to form a coalition with the left-socialists. Became head of the Third or Communist International in 1919.

party to plan for an armed seizure of power, against the wishes of leading Bolsheviks such as **Lev Kamenev** and **Gregori Zinoviev.**

Fundamentally, Lenin was powerful and skilful enough to subdue potential opposition within the Bolshevik Party at critical points in 1917. If he had failed to do so the Bolsheviks would never have been able to form a government.

Was Lenin merely an opportunist?

To Lenin the end justified the means. In *A Concise History of the Russian Revolution* (1995), the American historian, Richard Pipes, claims that Lenin treated politics like warfare. His opponents, both internal and external, had to be crushed by whatever means necessary. Robert Service discusses Lenin's **opportunism** in *Lenin: A Political Life – Volume 1* (1985):

Opportunism: the adaptation of one's actions and responses to take advantage of opportunities or circumstances.

'His ideas were amoeba-like, infinitely re-shapable. His attachment to the ultimate objectives of communism did not falter. He was not adverse to fudging issues and, on occasion, evading them altogether.'

Social and economic policy changes

One example of Lenin's inconsistency is the change that occurred in his attitude towards the Russian peasantry. In the 1890s Lenin believed that the basis of a Russian socialist state could be an alliance between the workers and peasants. However, by 1906 he had changed his views. In 'Two Tactics of Social Democracy' Lenin claimed that only poor peasants were suitable for alliance with the workers. Richer peasants, or 'kulaks', were seen as a major enemy of socialism. After 1917 Lenin supported a campaign against the kulaks.

Landmark Study The book that changed people's views

Robert Service, *Lenin: A Political Life* In Three Volumes; *Volume I: The Strengths of Contradiction* (Palgrave Macmillan, 1985) *Volume II: Worlds in Collision* (Palgrave Macmillan, 1991) *Volume III: The Iron Ring* (Palgrave Macmillan, 1995)

Robert Service, the British historian, has written a definitive political biography of Lenin. The first volume, covering Lenin's early life up to the First World War, was published just before the start of the Glasnost (openness) era of Mikhail Gorbachev. The second volume, covering 1914–18, was produced following the opening up of some of the Soviet archives to western historians. Finally, *The Iron Ring*, covering 1918–24, was written following the collapse of the USSR.

According to Robert Service, Lenin was over optimistic, underestimating Russian backwardness and the likelihood of a western-European socialist revolution. Lenin was also an opportunist. Lenin's failure to compromise damaged both the Bolsheviks and his own cause. Service believes that a socialist government combined of all socialist groups could have been set up in October 1917 without Lenin's participation. Lenin's determination to rule alone created a communist dictatorship.

Nationalisation: the process of placing industry, resources etc., under state control or ownership.

Lenin also supported wholesale state **nationalisation** of industry and the creation of collective farms for the peasants. During the Civil War, Lenin advocated the forceable seizure of grain and livestock from the peasants to feed the cities. This policy of War Communism lasted until the Tenth Party Congress in 1921 when, faced with widespread peasant opposition, Lenin modified his policy yet again. His New Economic Policy (1921–8) reversed War Communism and allowed peasants to sell surplus produce privately.

By the time of his death, Lenin's policies towards the major social groups in Russia had undergone several major changes. With the establishment of the USSR in 1922, the Soviet state was declared a republic of workers and peasants. However, it took Lenin's successor, Stalin, to create a truly socialist society by destroying an independent peasantry through forced **collectivisation** (1928–40).

Collectivisation: neighbouring peasants were forced to merge their lands into 'collective farms' called *Kolkozy*, in line with the Marxist principle of state ownership of the means of production.

Party political changes

Similarly, Lenin's policies were erratic in terms of party organisation. In her book *Lenin* (1999), Beryl Williams claims that he:

> 'seemed to contradict much of what he previously said. He now pressed for a large open party. Workers should be admitted in larger numbers, by hundreds and thousands without fearing them.'

This would seem to negate the very reason for the split from the RSDLP and the creation of a separate Bolshevik faction in 1903.

In addition, at the Fifth Party Congress in 1907 Lenin supported the idea that Bolsheviks should stand for and work with the State Duma, an idea contrary to his earlier support for all-out opposition to the Tsarist state. Possibly the greatest example of Lenin's opportunism though, is his change in attitude towards the Soviets. During the summer of 1917 he had called for 'All Power to the Soviets', yet once in power Lenin took the earliest opportunity to remove political power from the All Russia Soviet in order to create a Bolshevik dictatorship.

So was Lenin little more than an opportunist? Or did he have a clear aim to which he applied a number of different tactics to adapt to changing political conditions? During the Gorbachev era (1985–91) Lenin was hailed as an example of how to adapt communism to changing conditions, but perhaps the maxim of 'the end justifying the means' might still be justly applied in Lenin's case.

Was Lenin a help or hindrance to Russian socialism?

Lenin set out to take over the entire Russian Social Democratic Party, but failed in the attempt. From this perspective Lenin can be seen as a disruptive, divisive force, who sought ultimate power at the expense of socialist unity. At the Sixth Party Conference in Prague in 1912, Lenin tried to achieve a complete split between Bolsheviks and Mensheviks. Minutes of the meeting show that this move was bitterly resented by many Russian Bolsheviks. There is strong evidence to suggest that Bolsheviks and Mensheviks within Russia wanted to work together at both a local and a national level. Lenin's quest for complete control disrupted this process. In *Lenin's Path to Power* (1971), George Katkov and Harold Shukman maintain that:

> 'Throughout the period following the split of 1903 right up to 1917 there is a clearly discernible trend among Russian Social Democrats to make common cause and repair the breach between the two factions. Lenin is the outstanding exception.'

British historian, Robert Service, claims that Lenin's behaviour damaged the RSDLP and, subsequently, the Bolshevik Party. His refusal to compromise, coupled with his demand for total subservience from other socialist and Bolshevik leaders, caused endless friction.

In October 1917 the Bolsheviks were a minority group within Russia, so in order to sustain power, Lenin ruthlessly suppressed opponents, including Mensheviks and other non-Bolshevik socialists. Instead of helping to create a united socialist movement in Russia, Lenin's tactics ultimately destroyed the prospect of such a development and helped pave the way, not for a democratic socialist state, but for a Bolshevik dictatorship. In *The Origins of Bolshevism: The Intellectual Evolution of the Young Lenin* (1968), the American historian, Richard Pipes, asserts that:

'Lenin's strategy owed precious little to Marxism and everything to an insatiable lust for power.'

Q **Did Lenin help or hinder the development of Russian socialism?**

1. Read the following extract and answer the question.

'Lenin made his life-work the application of Marxism to the specific conditions of Russia. In him two worlds met: the native revolutionary tradition, springing from the necessities of Russian life and shaped by the structure of the Tsarist state. This was modified by scientific socialism and careful analysis of the class forces in a given situation, which Lenin derived from Marxism. Neither of the two traditions which met in Lenin had much in common with the parliamentary tradition which the Mensheviks wanted to transplant to the unsuitable soil of Russia.'

(adapted from Christopher Hill, *Lenin and the Russian Revolution* Hodder, 1970)

Using the information from the extract, and from this section, explain how Lenin adapted Marxism to Russian conditions in the years 1903 to October 1917.

2. To what extent did Lenin change his political ideas and the ways in which he planned to implement them between 1900 and October 1917?

2

Was the October Revolution a coup or mass uprising?

A Soviet view: history or propaganda?

Was the October Revolution really a coup by a small band of revolutionaries?

Did the Bolsheviks have popular support in October 1917?

Framework of events 1917

February	February Revolution
March	Tsar Nicholas II abdicated. End of monarchy
	Unofficial Committee of the Duma became Provisional Government
	Lenin wrote five *Letters from Afar* to Bolsheviks in Russia
April	Lenin returned to Petrograd and delivered his *April Theses*
	Demonstrations in Petrograd against Russian War aims
June	Demonstrations in Petrograd against June Offensive
July	July Days in Petrograd (3–5 July)
	Lenin fled to Finland
	Sixth Party Congress in Petrograd. Slogan 'All Power to the Soviets' abandoned
August	Kornilov Affair
October	Lenin returned to Petrograd
	Central Committee Meeting on armed seizure of power
	October Revolution (24–5 October): Bolsheviks seizure of power in Petrograd
	Lenin addressed Second Congress of All Russia Soviet

A Soviet view: history or propaganda?

Winter Palace: built in St Petersburg (1754–62) as the winter residence of the Tsars. After the February Revolution it became the headquarters of the Provisional Government.

In the 1920s the Soviet film director Sergei Eisenstein produced the silent film *October*, which showed thousands of Red Guards attacking the **Winter Palace** in Petrograd. The film suggested that the October Revolution, which overthrew the Provisional Government, was a popular mass uprising. This belief – one that dominated the thinking of successive Soviet governments up to the fall of the USSR in 1991 – was promoted for a number of reasons.

A freeze-frame from the film October by Sergei Eisenstein (1927), which was made for the tenth anniversary celebrations of the October Revolution. Lenin is shown standing on top of an armoured car during the storming of the Winter Palace.

Deification: to personify someone as God.

Mausoleum: a large and stately tomb usually constructed for a deceased leader.

Kremlin: the twelfth-century citadel in Moscow containing the former Imperial Palace and offices of the Russian government. Also (formerly) the central government of the Soviet Union.

At the time of Lenin's death, **Josef Stalin** and other communist leaders began to glorify Lenin as a great national leader. This **deification** of Lenin is apparent in the decision to preserve his body and put it on display in a large **mausoleum** in Red Square in Moscow, next to the **Kremlin**. In addition, Petrograd was renamed

Josef Stalin (1879–1953)
Adopted name of Josef Djugashvili. Stalin became a leading member of the Bolshevik Party and was active in the October Revolution, becoming People's Commissar for Nationalities in the first Soviet government. Was also General Secretary of the Bolshevik Party's Central Committee. After Lenin's death, Stalin took over the leadership of the Soviet Union.

'Peace, Bread, Land': Bolshevik slogan from April 1917. Reflected Bolshevik opposition to the war; the resolution of the food crisis in the towns; and the redistribution of land to the peasants.

Propaganda: information circulated to assist the cause of a government or movement.

Cold War: a conflict of military tension and political hostility between the USA and the USSR and their respective allies from the end of WWII until the collapse of the USSR in 1991.

Leningrad in his honour. Lenin was portrayed as the god-like genius who had foretold Russia's recent history. His slogans 'All Power to the Soviets' and **'Peace, Bread, Land'** had been supported by the Russian masses, therefore by October 1917 the Bolsheviks' seizure of power merely reflected the popular mood of the country.

Propaganda portraying the October uprising as a popular revolution was also important in legitimising the Soviet regime, which from 1917 attempted to declare itself the government supported by the population. From 1917 to 1945 the Soviet regime saw itself as the model for any future socialist society. Consequently, it was essential to develop the idea that the Bolshevik seizure of power was popular. In 1945 the Soviet Union became involved in a **Cold War** with the USA and the West and, with both sides trying to prove their superiority, the use of such propaganda became even more important.

To support their claim that the October Revolution was a popular one, Soviet historians intersperse their interpretation of events with political propaganda. Primarily they draw attention to the fact that the Bolsheviks won in an almost bloodless transfer of power. Indeed, very little support was shown to the outgoing Provisional Government. The Bolsheviks won power across Russia relatively easily, and when they dissolved the Constituent Assembly on 5 January 1918 after only one day, there was very little open opposition.

Was the October Revolution really a coup by a small band of revolutionaries?

What if the opposite to the Soviet view is true? What if the October Revolution was merely a conspiracy by a small group of revolutionaries acting against the wishes of the Russian people? This alternative interpretation was popular in the USA and the West during the Cold War, as it was convenient for western governments to portray the USSR as a repressive regime ruling not with, but in spite of, popular support. The rapid collapse of communism in eastern Europe in 1989 and in the USSR in 1991 seemed to confirm this view.

A major adherent of this view is American historian, Richard Pipes. In *The Russian Revolution, 1899–1919* (1990) he states:

'Although it is common to speak of two Russian revolutions in 1917 only one merits the name. In February 1917, Russia experienced a genuine revolution ... that brought down the Tsarist

Richard Pipes, *The Russian Revolution 1899–1919* (Harvill Press, 1990)

Pipes's 940-page work provides the basis for intense debate about the October Revolution. Pipes takes the view that Lenin was a ruthless, cowardly figure, who wished to gain dictatorial political power. He puts forward the case — held by many western historians during the Cold War — that the October Revolution was a conspiracy that ran counter to the wishes of the majority of the Russian people.

Pipes concentrates on the political history of the revolution, whereas other historians have emphasised the social and economic dimensions of the revolution and have taken a more generous view towards Lenin and the degree of popular support for the Bolsheviks. A major American critic of Pipes's approach is Ronald Grigor Suny in 'Revision and Retreat in the Historiography of 1917: a Social History and its Critics' in *Russian Review 53* (1994).

Nevertheless, Richard Pipes's study was the catalyst for a historical debate about October 1917 at the time of the collapse of the USSR.

regime. The Provisional Government that succeeded it gained immediate nationwide acceptance. Neither was true of October 1917. The events which led to the overthrow of the Provisional Government were not spontaneous but plotted and executed by a tightly organised conspiracy. October was a classic coup d'etat.'

In both the 1905 Revolution and the February Revolution of 1917, Bolsheviks played only a minor role. In fact both revolutions caught Lenin by surprise. In 1916 he told supporters in Switzerland, where he was in exile, that revolution in Russia was decades away and that it would be the next generation's task to fulfil what he had begun. It would appear that Lenin had become out of touch with conditions within Russia as, apart from a few months in 1905/6, he had been in foreign exile since 1900.

Both of the revolutions were unplanned, spontaneous reactions by the Russian people against political oppression and economic hardship. In fact, if any revolution was in the planning in February 1917, it came from the right wing of Russian politics, who favoured the removal of an incompetent Tsar in order to save the Tsarist political system.

When Lenin returned to Russia he did so with the support and assistance of Russia's wartime enemy, Germany. As Lenin supported the idea of a revolutionary civil war in which Russian workers were encouraged to overthrow the government, the Germans believed that he would assist them in destabilising the Russian government and war effort.

Sealed train: a train where the occupants are not allowed to get off the train until it reaches its destination.

Lenin was transported from Switzerland in a **sealed train**, which travelled via Germany and neutral Sweden to Russian Finland. The welcome he received from all revolutionaries upon his arrival at Petrograd late on the night of 3 April soon turned to uproar. From the top of an armoured car parked outside the station Lenin delivered a 90–minute speech on what became known as his *April Theses*. Lenin denounced the Provisional Government as reactionary and demanded its overthrow, a view that ran counter to those held by the Russian Bolshevik leadership, headed by Kamenev and Stalin.

From the moment he returned to Russia Lenin planned to overthrow the Provisional Government, which he attempted on three occasions before his eventual seizure of power in October 1917.

The April Theses

Published in *Pravda* on 7 April 1917

- The war is a greedy war for territory and should be ended immediately.

- The revolution ... is to move to its second stage, which must place power in the hands of the proletariat and the poorest peasants.

- No support for the Provisional Government.

- The masses must be made to see that the Soviet is ... the only possible form of revolutionary government.

- Abolition of the police, the army and the bureaucracy. The salaries of all officials should not exceed the average wage of a worker.

- Confiscation of all landed estates from the landowners and aristocracy.

- Mass propaganda to win over peasants and workers.

- The immediate union of all banks in the country into a single national bank.

- All production of goods to come under Soviet control.

- An international organisation to be set up to spread revolution worldwide.

What strategies did Lenin use to attempt the overthrow of the Provisional Government in 1917?

On 21 April Lenin attempted to topple the Provisional Government through mass demonstrations, using the catalyst of mass discontent over the government's commitment to continue in the war. The Bolshevik Central Committee even issued an order to send agitators to factories and barracks to persuade workers and soldiers to join in any demonstrations, but they were easily dispersed.

Again on 9 June, the Bolsheviks attempted to exploit the Provisional Government's lack of popularity in order to bring about its downfall. This time the pretext was disillusionment with a major Russian offensive on the Eastern Front. Yet all attempts to persuade the Petrograd Soviet and the Congress of Soviets to support such a move failed and a Bolshevik coup was averted.

The July Days

The events of the July Days have provoked harsh criticism of Lenin. To Richard Pipes:

> 'no event in the Russian Revolution has been more wilfully lied about … the reason being that it was Lenin's worst blunder, a misjudgement that nearly caused the destruction of the Bolshevik Party: the equivalent of Hitler's 1923 beer-hall putsch. To absolve themselves of responsibility, the Bolsheviks have gone to unusual lengths to misrepresent the July putsch as a spontaneous demonstration which they sought to direct into peaceful channels.'

The pretext of the July Days had been to move some of the Petrograd garrison to the front. This was following the failure of the Russian June offensive, which had provoked fear of a German counter-offensive against the capital. On 4 July the pro-Bolshevik Machine Gun Regiment and the Red Guards occupied key points in the city. They were joined by 5000–6000 sailors from the Kronstadt naval base and later 10 000 workers from the Putilov factory. But just when it looked as though Lenin finally had Petrograd in his grasp, he lost his nerve and fled to Finland.

Opposition to Lenin further developed when the government claimed he was acting as an agent of the Germans and was receiving financial assistance from them. On 6 July Lenin and ten other Bolsheviks were charged with 'high treason and organising an armed uprising'. Altogether 800 were arrested and a few days later both Lenin and Zinoviev fled the city.

This photo of Lenin in disguise was taken for the false papers he used in order to return to Russia without fear of arrest. Lenin hid in friends' apartments throughout October.

In her book, *Lenin* (1999), Beryl Williams cites the July Days as a turning point. Lenin and the Bolsheviks had attempted a takeover but had failed miserably and, after July, the initiative to threaten the government seemed to pass from Lenin's hands.

**Leon Trotsky
(1879–1940)**
Born Lev Davidovitch Bronstein. Became involved in revolutionary activities as a teenager and was exiled to Siberia. Escaped in 1902 and joined the Social Democrats. Trotsky was initially critical of Lenin, but joined the Bolsheviks in May 1917 and played a major role in the October Revolution. Founder and Supreme Commander of the Red Army.

What led the Bolsheviks to call for an armed seizure of power?

In August, the Kornilov Affair raised the fear of a right-wing coup, which took pressure off the Bolsheviks. The Provisional Government armed the workers of Petrograd, and Bolshevik support increased dramatically. In Lenin's absence, power over the Red Guards fell to **Leon Trotsky**, and it was he who engaged in the initial plan for an armed seizure of power.

Also of considerable significance in moving the Bolsheviks towards armed insurrection was an announcement by the Provisional Government on 9 August, proposing a timetable for national elections to a Constituent Assembly. The elections would be on 12 November with the opening session on 28 November. Lenin was well aware that in such an election the SRs would be the largest political force, so any armed seizure of power would have to take place before that date.

Lenin's tactics over the summer offered a way forward. Following his return to Russia he advocated the transferral of all political power to the All Russia Soviet. Lenin knew that the Bolsheviks did not have a chance to participate in and influence the Provisional Government, but they could, and did, rapidly increase their participation in regional soviets and the All Russia Soviet. Support for the Bolsheviks grew because they were the only major group in opposition to an increasingly unpopular Provisional Government. They were also popular for their call for 'Peace, Bread and Land', although some saw this slogan as a cynical attempt to win support.

The catalyst for the seizure of power on 24 October came not from Lenin but from the Provisional Government, which attempted to close down two Bolshevik newspapers. With the help of Trotsky, Lenin was able to persuade the Central Committee of the Party to accept the idea of an armed uprising. Using the Military Revolutionary Committee (MRC) of the Petrograd Soviet, the Bolsheviks planned to capture Petrograd on the eve of the Second Congress of the All Russia Soviet. Then, when they had seized power, they would announce they had done so on behalf of the Soviet. On the evenings of 24 and 25 October, MRC units and Red Guards occupied key areas of Petrograd, arrested the Provisional Government, and declared a new government the following day.

An interpretation of the storming of the Winter Palace by the Soviet artist Sokolov-Skaljal (1939).

How was a small conspiratorial group able to seize power in the world's largest country?

The answer lies in the chaotic conditions existing in Russia during 1917: economic hardship caused by the war; low levels of morale in the army, particularly after the failure of the June Offensive; and the breakdown of law and order in the countryside. The Bolsheviks were best placed to take advantage of this chaos as they were a centralised, disciplined party which had distanced itself from the Provisional Government. According to Orlando Figes in *A People's Tragedy* (1996), with their slogan of 'Peace, Bread, Land', the Bolsheviks deliberately undermined the authority of the Provisional Government, thus hastening its collapse.

Even though Bolsheviks were in the minority across the country as a whole, they gave the appearance of acting for the majority in the All Russia and Petrograd Soviet. In fact, at no time during 1917 did the Bolsheviks have majority support within Russia: their appeal was strongest amongst town dwellers and in sections of the armed forces. In the Constituent Assembly elections of November 1917 the Bolsheviks achieved only 24 per cent of the vote.

Alexei Rykov (1881–1938)
Joined the Bolsheviks in 1903 but mistrusted Lenin and secretly supported plans for coalition government in 1917. People's Commissar for the Interior 1917–18; Politburo member (1924–9); Chairman of the Supreme Council for the National Economy 1918–20 and 1923–4. Elected to succeed Lenin as Chairman of the Sovnarkom and Prime Minister of the USSR. Leading supporter of the NEP.

It has also been suggested that the very nature of the Bolshevik Party implied a conspiracy of a minority. In *What is to be Done?* Lenin recommended that the RSDLP should be restricted to a small group of professional revolutionaries, who would plan for the seizure of power in Russia on behalf of the industrial working class and peasantry.

Lenin deliberately used popular support for the All Russia Soviet to mask the Bolshevik plan to seize power. As historian, Leonard Schapiro states in *The Communist Party of the Soviet Union,* (1960):

'the soviets rather than the party attracted mass allegiance, which the Bolsheviks exploited.'

However, once in power Lenin had no desire to share power with the All Russia Soviet or with any other socialist party, except the Left SRs for a short period (December 1917 to March 1918). Support for the All Russia Soviet simply provided a smokescreen for a conspiracy.

Further evidence confirming this comes from a study of what the Bolsheviks did once they achieved power. Most representatives in the All Russia Soviet hoped that the Bolsheviks would form a coalition government, but Lenin planned to rule alone, and maintained power through the use of political terror and repression. The leading Bolsheviks Kamenev, Zinoviev and **Alexei Rykov** believed that if the Bolsheviks did not create a coalition socialist government, they would only be able to rule through terror.

Did the Bolsheviks have popular support in October 1917?

Richard Pipes's work has generated considerable historical debate about the nature of the October Revolution. However, whilst his study concentrates on the political history of the Revolution, it fails to take into account the social and economic conditions of the time. Critics of Pipes's perspective point out that, in the late summer and autumn of 1917, Russia was in a state of social turmoil: peasants were seizing land and individual nationalist groups were asserting their independence. Historians from John Keep in *Russian Revolution: A Study in Mass Mobilisation* (1976) to French historian Marc Ferro in *October 1917: A Social History of the Russian Revolution* (1980), who have concentrated on the social aspects of 1917, agree that disillusionment with the war and economic collapse meant that the Bolsheviks did indeed have widespread popular support.

The Constituent Assembly election results show the Bolsheviks polling 25 per cent of the popular vote. They achieved majority support amongst the urban working class and from over ten per cent of the peasantry. The SR vote is somewhat misleading as it does not differentiate between SRs and Left SRs, the latter of which formed a significant minority and joined the Bolsheviks in government in December 1917.

Many hoped that, once in power, the Bolsheviks would form a coalition government of socialist groups. Consequently, when this failed to materialise, support drifted away to the point that the Bolsheviks were forced to rule through terror.

Election Results for the Constituent Assembly, November 1917

	% of vote
Socialist Revolutionaries	40.4
Bolsheviks	24
Mensheviks	2.6
Left Socialist Revolutionaries	1
Other socialist parties	0.9
Kadets (Liberals)	4.7
Other liberal groups	2.8
National minority parties	13.4
Results not known	10.2

(From *The Russian Revolution 1899–1919* by Richard Pipes (1990)

Why did support for the Bolsheviks increase?

By October the Bolshevik Party was no longer a small, close-knit body of professional revolutionaries. According to historian Christopher Read, in *From Tsar to Soviets: Russian People and their Revolution, 1917–21* (1996), Bolshevik membership rose from 10 000 in February to over 200 000 in October. Similarly, in *Rethinking the Russian Revolution* (1990), Edward Acton claims that membership numbers climbed from 24 000 to 350 000. By September 1917 the Bolsheviks were publishing 75 different newspapers and journals in eight different languages, and the print-run of the party newspaper *Pravda* (Truth) had increased from 90 000 in July to 200 000 in October.

Other reasons for the increased support for the Bolsheviks include the openness associated with the fall of the Tsar; the creation of the Provisional Government; and their demands for the end of the war and the distribution of land to the peasants. The Bolshevik slogan of 'Peace, Bread, Land' mirrored the views of the majority of the Russian people.

Bolshevik support rose most rapidly amongst the urban working class (proletariat), the social group around which Lenin had planned the socialist revolution. Bolshevik support also increased in factory committees as well as local soviets.

In *The Russian Revolution, 1917* (2000), Rex Wade states:

'The Russian Revolution of 1917 was a number of concurrent and overlapping revolutions: a popular revolt against the old regime; a workers' revolt against the hardships of the old industrial and social order; a revolt by soldiers against the old system of military service and then against the war; a peasants' evolution for land and control of their own lives; middle class elements and educated society for civil rights and parliamentary government and a revolt of most of the people against the war and slaughter.'

The Bolshevik's position seemed to attract many, if not all, of these groups.

What advantages did the Bolsheviks have over other political parties?

As 1917 progressed, the Bolsheviks developed a number of advantages over other parties and groups. They had a recognised leader, Lenin, who had made clear his implacable opposition to the Provisional Government and its policies, and they had a Central

Irakli Tsereteli (1881–1960) A Russian socialist who became a leading Menshevik after the 1903 RSDLP split and was editor of the Menshevik paper *Kvali* (Track). Minister of the Interior in the Provisional Government. After the October Revolution Lenin ordered Tsereteli's arrest so he remained in Georgia throughout the Civil War. When the Red Army captured the area he fled to France and later emigrated to the USA.

Committee, which offered a clear decision-making apparatus as well as a core of dedicated supporters forming the basis for growth.

Revolutionary defencism: policy associated with the Menshevik leadership of Tsereteli and Fedor Dan from February 1917. They opposed offensive operations in the war but were willing to fight if the Germans attacked the Russian army.

There is also the issue of divisions in opposition groups. The Mensheviks were linked with the idea of **revolutionary defencism** – associated with their leader, **Irakli Tsereteli** – which became increasing unpopular after the failure of the June Offensive. Tsereteli had been in the Provisional Government from May, and this compromised his position with left-wing supporters, who looked to the founder of Menshevism, Yuli Martov, for alternative leadership.

Similarly, the SRs were compromised when their leader, Victor Chernov, also joined the Provisional Government in May. Growing opposition to the Provisional Government's agricultural policy was shown at the SR council, which took place between 6 and 10 August. Left SRs received 40 per cent of the vote and were eventually to join Lenin's government in December 1917.

Finally, with the creation of the Third Provisional Government, under **Alexander Kerensky,** on 25 September, central authority within Russia had all but collapsed. Following the failure of the June Offensive, the Kornilov Affair, and the rapid economic collapse of the country, Russia simply lacked effective government. The Bolsheviks did not have to seize power, but merely fill a vacuum left by an inept and increasingly ignored Provisional Government.

Alexander Kerensky (1881–1970) Successively Minister of Justice, War Minister and Prime Minister of the Provisional Government in 1917. By coincidence Kerensky was born in the same town as Lenin and his father was headmaster of the school that Lenin attended.

Was the October Revolution a coup or mass uprising?

1. Read the following extract and then answer the question.

   'The Bolshevik Revolution was anything but popular and democratic. The party was and remained a conspiratorial minority, whose active membership 'consisted in the main of intellectuals'. Their success can be explained in the first instance by their superior organisation. A highly centralised body of professional revolutionaries had been Lenin's ideal since he wrote 'What is to be Done?' in 1902. The tightly-knit, military style organisation he created stood in stark contrast to its feeble, fractured, ill-organized rivals.'

   (adapted from Edward Acton, *Rethinking the Russian Revolution* Hodder Arnold, 1990)

   Using the information in the extract above, and from this section, how far do you agree with the suggestion that the October Revolution was a coup by an unrepresentative minority?

2. *'The Bolsheviks did not gain power in October 1917, they merely filled a vacuum left by the disintegration of the Provisional Government'.*

   Assess the validity of this view.

3 Lenin: liberator or dictator? The Bolsheviks in power 1917–24

How did he stay in power after October 1917?

How far did he change the Russian government, economy and society?

Was his attempt to export the revolution a complete failure?

Framework of events

1917	Lenin addressed Second Congress of All Russia Soviet
	Bolshevik government (Sovnarkom) formed
	Elections to Constituent Assembly
	Bolsheviks called for armistice (ceasefire) on Eastern Front, which came into effect on 2 December
1918	Constituent Assembly dissolved by Bolsheviks
	Treaty of Brest-Litovsk
	Capital moved from Petrograd to Moscow
	Party name changed to Communist Party
	Introduction of War Communism
	Start of Left SR uprising
	Official creation of Russian Soviet Federative Soviet Republic
1919	First Comintern Congress
	Turning point in Civil War against the Whites
1920	Russo-Polish War
1921	End of Civil War
	Kronstadt Mutiny
	War Communism abandoned and NEP introduced
1922	Creation of USSR
	Lenin suffered two strokes
1924	Lenin died

I n *History of Russia: The Bolshevik Revolution, Part 1* (1960) the English historian, Edward H. Carr, declares that Lenin's greatest achievement was not in gaining political power, but in keeping it.

The problems facing Lenin were daunting. Alongside his promise to remove Russia from the First World War, Lenin also had to deal with a complete national breakdown in law and order. All of this was happening at a time of severe economic crisis when, to make matters worse, the old Russian Empire seemed to be disintegrating; minorities such as Finns, Ukrainians and Georgians were setting up their own governments.

In addition to these problems, Lenin was faced with the enormous task of creating a socialist society within Russia. Lenin hoped that social revolution in Russia would coincide with a worldwide socialist revolution. His lasting wish was to see socialist revolution take place in western Europe, in particular in Britain and Germany.

How did Lenin stay in power after October 1917?

According to Karl Marx, once a socialist revolution had taken place in an advanced industrial economy it would be followed by a 'dictatorship of the proletariat (industrial working class)', who would constitute the majority of the population. However, in the Russia of 1917 this was impossible as 80 per cent of the population were peasants. Also, Lenin believed that a Bolshevik dictatorship should act as the representative of the Russian working class.

How did Lenin remove opposition from within his own party?

From the moment that Lenin seized power he was determined to rule. In *A People's Tragedy: The Russian Revolution 1891–1924* (1996), Orlando Figes cites Lenin's determination to establish not only a Bolshevik dictatorship of Russia, but also a personal dictatorship over the Bolshevik Party itself. As Figes notes:

> 'Lenin's bullying tactics would soon lead to a situation where only one man would be left in the Party – the Dictator … This was without doubt one of the most critical moments in the history of the Bolshevik Party.'

An example of Lenin's desire to establish supreme control came on 4 November 1917, when five moderate Bolsheviks – including Kamenev, Zinoviev and Rykov – resigned from the Party's Central

Committee after being accused of holding talks with other socialist parties. Lenin also set about purging their supporters from the Central Committee.

Yet even this ruthless approach did not enable Lenin to totally eradicate internal dissent, or mean that he was completely unwilling to work with other parties for tactical reasons. In fact, from December 1917 to March 1918, Lenin agreed to a coalition with the Left SRs, although they were always treated as a minority.

Internal conflict was an important factor in leading Lenin to ban all factions within the Bolshevik/Communist Party at the Tenth Party Congress in March 1921. From 1921 the Party followed a policy of 'democratic centralism' whereby there was open discussion and debate on matters of policy but, once a decision had been made by the Party leadership, all members were expected to follow that decision unquestioningly. In this way Lenin had created a political dictatorship.

How did Lenin deal with external challenges?

The greatest external threat to Lenin's rule came from the Constituent Assembly elections, which were virtually a referendum on Bolshevik rule. It was impossible for Lenin to cancel the elections without provoking widespread unrest. When the results were counted, the Bolsheviks had achieved only 24 per cent of the vote – amounting to approximately 10 million votes – mainly from workers and soldiers. Of vital importance however, was the Bolshevik majorities in Petrograd and Moscow, where they won 175 seats out of a total of 715.

When the Constituent Assembly met on 5 January 1918 in the Tauride Palace, Petrograd, the Bolsheviks demanded the subservience of the Assembly to decrees from the All Russia Soviet and Sovnarkom (the Russian Government). When this was rejected by 237 votes to 137 the Bolsheviks and Left SRs withdrew and Lenin

Landmark Study   **The book that changed people's views**

Orlando Figes, *A People's Tragedy: The Russian Revolution 1891–1924* (Jonathan Cape, 1996)

This award-winning text provides a revision of the views of previous historians on Lenin, in particular, Richard Pipes. *A People's Tragedy* presents the results of Figes's previous research into peasant attitudes towards Bolshevik rule, contained in his other works entitled

Peasant Russia, Civil War: The Volga Countryside in Revolution, (1917–1921) (1989) and 'The Red Army and Mass Mobilisation during the Russia Civil War' in *Past and Present* (1990).

In the wake of the collapse of the USSR and the opening up of Russian

archives, this study provides a benchmark in western interpretation, not only of Lenin's rule from 1917, but also of the whole process of revolution in Russia from the last decade of the nineteenth century.

Fedor Dan (1871–1947)
A Russian writer and physician who became a Menshevik and a member of the Petrograd Soviet after the February Revolution, supporting the Provisional Government. Dan was an infamous opponent of Lenin and was expelled for inciting counter-revolution in 1922.

dissolved the assembly. According to American historian, Richard Pipes, in *The Russian Revolution, 1899–1919* (1990):

> 'the dispersal of the Constituent Assembly was in many respects more important for the future of Russia than the October coup. There can be no doubt about Bolshevik intentions after January 5th, when they made it unmistakably clear they intended to pay no heed to public opinion.'

The main reason the Bolsheviks succeeded was that the opposition parties were struggling with their own internal conflicts. The SRs were split, the Left SRs having joined the Bolsheviks in government in December 1917. The leader of the majority SRs, Victor Chernov, called for a peaceful demonstration following dissolution, but this was easily handled by the Bolshevik Red Guards. The Mensheviks were also divided between followers of **Fedor Dan** and followers of Martov, and were only reunited in May 1918.

In the wake of the dissolution, opposition to the Bolsheviks within the civil service collapsed. It was indeed a major turning point in their creation of a dictatorship.

The Treaty of Brest-Litovsk, 3 March 1918

The greatest amount of dissent within the Party was caused by the signing of The Treaty of Brest-Litovsk: a peace treaty between Russia, Germany and Austria-Hungary. True to their demand for 'Peace', the Bolsheviks negotiated a ceasefire (armistice) on the Eastern Front two weeks after the October Revolution. The leading Bolshevik negotiator in this was Leon Trotsky, who used the peace talks to spread Bolshevik propaganda among German and Austro-Hungarian troops.

The Bolsheviks were forced to sign an extremely harsh peace, following the decision by the German High Command to renew their military operations on 18 February. Russia had to surrender Courland (Estonia), Latvia, Lithuania, Poland and the Ukraine, which amounted to 34 per cent of the population, 32 per cent of agricultural land and 54 per cent of industry.

Lenin supported the Treaty because he believed that without it the Bolsheviks would lose the Civil War that had broken out following their seizure of power. However, the decision to accept the Treaty was only carried by a single vote and, as an immediate consequence, the coalition with the Left SRs came to an end.

Russian territory lost in
the Treaty of Brest-
Litovsk, March 1918.

How did the Bolsheviks win the Civil War 1918–21?

Lenin's greatest triumph was to win the Civil War. Yet there is some
dispute about when the Civil War actually began. It could be argued

Cossack: cavalry troops
from southern Russia.
Usually supporters of the
Whites in the Civil War.

that it started with the defeat of **Cossack** forces outside Petrograd
on 1 November 1917, but it was clearly underway by the signing of
the Treaty of Brest Litovsk on 3 March 1918.

Traditionally, the Civil War has been seen as a conflict between
the Reds (Bolsheviks) and the Whites (anti-Bolsheviks). However,
the conflict was much more complex:

● From 1918 to 1919 several foreign powers intervened in the
  Civil War: Britain, France, the USA, Japan and Italy, all of whom
  supported the anti-Bolshevik forces.

- The Czech Legion (Czech POWs from the Austro-Hungarian army), numbering 26 000, played an important part in fighting the Bolsheviks in Siberia in 1918.

- There were also conflicts with the Greens: peasant armies who fought both with and against the Bolsheviks at various times.

- National groups seeking independence. These included Finns, Estonians, Ukrainians and Georgians.

So there were several civil wars within the Russian Civil War. From November 1917 to 1920 the Bolsheviks fought the Whites, who were usually ex-Tsarists. From March to August 1918 the Bolsheviks fought the Left SRs. From 1920 to 1921 the Bolsheviks fought the Greens and the Poles.

The Bolsheviks won for a variety of reasons:

- They controlled the heartland of Russia from Petrograd to Moscow and Tsaritsyn (now Volgograd), which included most of the Russian population.

- Bolshevik propaganda portrayed Whites as anti-Russian and willing to return Russia to Tsarist rule.

The Russian Civil War and foreign intervention 1918–21.

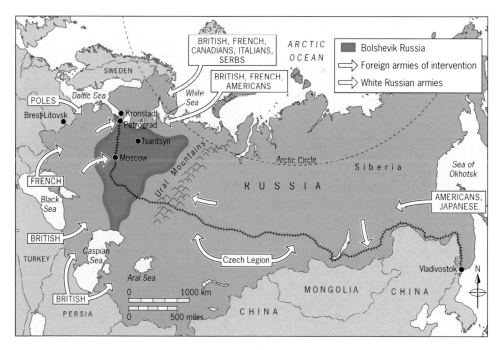

- They had an effective centralised leadership, unlike the Whites, who lacked central coordination and clear policy aims, allowing the Reds to defeat them in turn.

- Leon Trotsky set up the Red Army using ex-Tsarist officers and conscription. The Red Army numbered five million by 1921.

- The Allied intervention was very limited and was reduced following the end of the First World War.

The use of political terror

Terror: the deliberate use of arrest, imprisonment and execution to enforce political control. The Red Terror began in earnest in the summer of 1918, at the height of the Civil War. Its most famous victims were the Russian royal family, who were murdered in July 1918 at Ekaterinburg in Siberia.

The most controversial aspect of Lenin's rule was his use of political terror. Apologists for Lenin claim that, confronted with massive economic crisis and counter-revolution, he had little alternative but to use **terror** against opponents and that, once the immediate crisis was over, political terror would subside. This is central to the official Soviet view put forward by works such as *A Short History of the Communist Party of the Soviet Union* (1970). Institutionalised, permanent terror is more associated with Stalin's regime (1924–53).

The Bolsheviks placed great emphasis on history. In the French Revolution (1792–4) political terror was used at times of political and economic crisis to ensure the survival of the revolution. Using this historical parallel, Lenin justified employing such tactics to guarantee the survival of the Bolshevik Revolution. This opinion is shared by Dmitri Volkogonov in *Lenin, Life and Legacy* (1994). A Colonel General in the Soviet armed forces, Volkogonov was also Director of the Institute of Military History in the 1980s and had access to its archives. He believes that 'Lenin cannot be accused of personal cruelty. The main argument for the terror was to protect the working class.' Faced with an acute crisis in 1918–21: famine, factories on strike, a breakdown in law and order, peasants hiding grain, and the army in disintegration, Lenin saw terror as the only thing that would save the country from collapse.

However, the British historian, Robert Service, takes the view that Lenin 'continued to lean in favour of dictatorship and terror'. Indeed Trotsky himself stated that Lenin believed in the use of terror 'at every suitable opportunity'. Richard Pipes goes further saying:

> 'the Red Terror constituted from the outset an essential element of the regime. It never disappeared hanging like a permanent cloud over Soviet Russia.'

Cheka members on the march

The Cheka

Felix Dzerzhinky (1877–1926)
A Polish communist revolutionary, Dzerzkinsky joined the Bolsheviks in 1917 and was founder of the Bolshevik security police, the Cheka. His honesty and devotion to the cause earned him the nickname 'Iron Felix'. Later Minister for the Interior and for Communications and head of the Supreme Council of the National Economy.

The use of terror began early in Lenin's regime. The Military Revolutionary Committee (MRC) of the Petrograd Soviet had a specific section to tackle counter-revolution, headed by **Felix Dzerzhinsky**. On 6 December 1917 Sovnarkom established the Cheka (The All Russia Extraordinary Commission for the Suppression of Counter Revolution and Sabotage). This was a major departure from the policies of the Provisional Government, who had abolished the Okhrana (Tsarist secret police) and the death penalty after the February Revolution.

The Cheka's main purpose was to arrest, imprison and execute political opponents but, in A *People's Tragedy; The Russian Revolution 1891–1924* (1996), Figes highlights a further motive for the creation of such a group. He sees it as part of a general war on privilege, the Orthodox Church and the wealthy. Figes also points out that the Red Terror actually intensified opposition to the Bolsheviks during the Civil War.

The Cheka existed from December 1917 to February 1922. At the US Senate Judiciary Committee hearings in 1971, British historian, Robert Conquest, claimed the Cheka had been responsible for 500 000 executions and deaths. In *Lenin, Terror and the Political Order* (1975), G. Leggat puts the figure closer to 140 000, but in either case these figures far exceed the reputed 14 000 killed by the Okhrana under the Tsars.

Defenders of Lenin stress the fact that he disbanded the Cheka in February 1922 as soon the crisis of Civil War was over. However, the abolition of the Cheka was simply a 'cosmetic exercise' according to Robert Service, as it was immediately replaced by the GPU (Main Political Administration), attached to the People's Commissariat of Internal Affairs. Whilst moderate Bolsheviks/Communists such as Lev Kamenev had attempted to limit the terror by this reform, in reality Lenin secured its continuance, laying the foundations for the terror regime of his successor, Stalin.

How far did Lenin change the Russian government, economy and society?

How Russia was governed under Lenin

Lenin created a completely new type of government following the October Revolution. Because of its association with the Tsarist regime, the term 'minister' was replaced by 'commissar'. With Lenin as chair, the Council of People's Commissars (Sovnarkom) formed the Russian government.

Sovnarkom shared political power with the All Russia Soviet but, following rigged elections to the Third Congress of the All Russia Soviet in January 1918, the Soviet and its regional counterparts lost political influence. In January 1918, and confirmed on July 1918, Russia received a **federal constitution**. However, this existed in name only. Real power lay with the Bolshevik/Communist Party. Soviet Russia was a centralised state with Lenin as its dictator.

Federal constitution: a system of government where states are united and have a central government but considerable power and authority is given to the individual states.

At the Eighth Party Congress in March 1919, the Politburo was created. This committee acted on behalf of the Central Committee of the Communist Party. It replaced Sovnarkom as the main decision making body. It originally contained five members: Lenin, Trotsky, Kamenev, Stalin and Party Secretary, Krestinsky.

Social and economic policy changes

The creation of the Bolshevik regime was meant to usher in a completely new type of society: the world's first communist state. However, one major obstacle was that Russia was a country where 80 per cent of the population were peasants. According to Edward Acton in *Rethinking the Russian Revolution* (1990), another difficulty faced by Lenin was that:

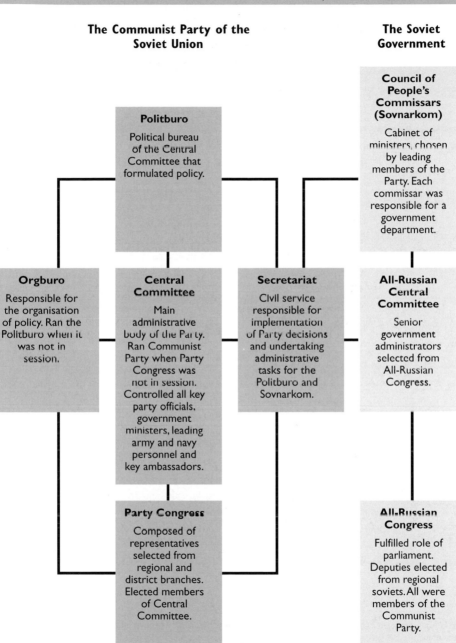

The Communist Party of the Soviet Union

The Soviet Government

Council of People's Commissars (Sovnarkom)

Cabinet of ministers, chosen by leading members of the Party. Each commissar was responsible for a government department.

Politburo

Political bureau of the Central Committee that formulated policy.

Orgburo

Responsible for the organisation of policy. Ran the Politburo when it was not in session.

Central Committee

Main administrative body of the Party. Ran Communist Party when Party Congress was not in session. Controlled all key party officials, government ministers, leading army and navy personnel and key ambassadors.

Secretariat

Civil service responsible for implementation of Party decisions and undertaking administrative tasks for the Politburo and Sovnarkom.

All-Russian Central Committee

Senior government administrators selected from All-Russian Congress.

Party Congress

Composed of representatives selected from regional and district branches. Elected members of Central Committee.

All-Russian Congress

Fulfilled role of parliament. Deputies elected from regional soviets. All were members of the Communist Party.

The political structure of the Soviet Union in the mid 1920s.

'in the aftermath of the October Revolution the country suffered an economic collapse on the scale of a modern Black Death. 60 per cent of the workforce were unemployed by mid 1918. Petrograd lost 1 million inhabitants following the October Revolution.'

And all this was taking place with a background of Civil War from 1918 to 1921.

War Communism 1918

Lenin's first aim was to create a 'commune state', with decentralised control of factories and farms by workers and peasants respectively. This only lasted for a few months after the October Revolution, as in December 1917 it was replaced by a completely opposite approach: wholesale state nationalisation of factories. By 1921 economic conditions in Russia were so bad that famine was widespread. By the end of 1922 over three million had died of starvation and disease and outbreaks of cannibalism were even reported.

In June 1918 a further policy was introduced. Referred to at the time as 'Communism' it became known as War Communism. Soviet interpretations suggested that War Communism was a temporary policy brought about by the demands of the Civil War, but Lenin hoped it would form the basis of the Russian economy. Industrial production was planned through central planning offices run by the government. To control agriculture, Narkomprod (People's Commissariat for Foodstuffs) was created to organise local commit-tees of poor peasants. These committees were to prove a failure, however. With cities short of food, Lenin resorted to using the Urals-Siberian method of grain procurement; gangs of Bolsheviks were sent to the countryside to forcibly take grain from the peasants. In factories industrial conscription was introduced and 'storm troops' of Bolsheviks were organised to boost industrial production.

The effects of War Communism were catastrophic. Peasant uprisings broke out across Russia. By 1920 iron production had dropped to one twelfth of what it had been in 1918 and, by October 1920, the Russian currency – the rouble – was valued at just one per cent of its October 1917 value. The economy only seemed to function at all through the **Black Market**. By March 1921 Lenin's attempt to introduce a socialist-style economy was in ruins.

Black Market: illegal private trading.

Lenin's New Economic Policy 1921

Lenin faced a major crisis in March 1921 with the economy on the verge of collapse. Large parts of the country were suffering peasant uprisings and, between 8 and 18 March the sailors of the Kronstadt naval base near Petrograd rose in rebellion against what they saw as the broken promises of Lenin's government. Trotsky only managed to suppress the mutiny with great ferocity.

Against this background the Tenth Party Congress met. Lenin announced the abandonment of War Communism, replacing it with a New Economic Policy (NEP). The NEP allowed private ownership

Reforms passed by the Bolsheviks 1917–18

The Decree on Land, 26 October 1917

Abolished private ownership of land by wealthy landowners, merely recognising what had already taken place in the countryside. Lenin favoured the creation of collective farms rather than private peasant farms.

The Decree on Peace, 26 October 1917

Proposed a three-month armistice. Transmitted to Allied governments on 9 November.

The Decree on the Press, 27 October 1917

The 'counter-revolutionary press' (papers that criticised the Bolsheviks) was to be closed.

Declaration of the Rights of the Toiling and Exploited Masses, 8 January 1918

- abolished private property

- nationalised the banks

- founded Vesenka, the Supreme Economic Council

- introduced labour conscription.

The Creation of the Russian Soviet Federative Soviet Republic (RSFSR), January 1918

Declared Russia to be 'a republic of soviets of workers', soldiers' and peasants' deputies' and a 'free union of free nations, a federation of Soviet Republics'.

Industrial and agricultural production in millions of tons (except electricity)

	1913	1920	1921	1922	1923	1924	1925	1926
Grain	80.0	46.0	37.0	50.0	57.0	51.0	72.0	77.0
Coal	29.0	8.7	8.9	9.5	13.7	16.1	18.1	27.6
Steel	4.2	–	0.2	0.4	0.7	1.1	2.1	3.1
Iron	4.2	–	0.1	0.2	0.3	0.7	1.5	2.4
Electricity (mill KWhs)	1945	–	520	775	1146	1562	2925	3508

The effects of War Communism and the NEP on production levels.

of small firms (those employing fewer than 20 people) and, more importantly, it ended forcible grain requisitioning and allowed peasants to sell their grain on the private market. Large scale industry remained under state control, however. Lenin declared that 'only an agreement with the peasants will save the Russian Revolution until other revolutions break out somewhere else'. In social and economic terms this was a backwards step for communism. Lenin had created a state of workers and peasants (represented

**ТОВ. Ленин ОЧИЩАЕТ
землю от нечисти.**

'Comrade Lenin sweeps away the world's dirt' a propaganda poster produced in 1920.

by the state symbol of the hammer and sickle), but it was left to Stalin to accomplish a total social and economic revolution.

Was Lenin's attempt to export the revolution a complete failure?

To Lenin, socialist revolution was a worldwide phenomenon; the seizure of power in Russia was merely a prelude to the spread of revolution across the world. In line with his thinking in *Imperialism, the Highest Stage of Capitalism* (1916), revolution began in Russia as it was capitalism's weakest link. Like other Marxists, Lenin believed that socialism would only take permanent root in Russia with help from other advanced industrialised countries. The universal aim of world socialism was reflected in the name of the new state created in 1922. The Union of Soviet Socialist Republics had no geographical limitation in its title. Ultimately, the whole world would be in the USSR.

In 1918/9 the prospect of exporting the socialist revolution seemed promising but, as the severe strain of the First World War began to tell, riots and strikes affected many of the participants and, by November 1918 the Austro-Hungarian Empire was in the process of disintegration. In January 1919 the **Spartacist** Revolt took place in Berlin. In 1919 a Soviet-style republic was created in Bavaria, and Hungary became the Hungarian Socialist Republic. Yet these attempts at socialist revolution were short-lived and all had failed by the end of 1919. Elsewhere in Europe – in Britain and Italy – widespread industrial unrest occurred in the two years following the war.

Spartacists: a movement founded in 1916 and reorganised as the German Communist Party in November 1918. Aimed to overthrow capitalism by a revolutionary rising of German workers. All attempts were suppressed.

The Third Communist International (Comintern)

To encourage a global socialist revolution Lenin set up Comintern in March 1919, under the presidency of Gregori Zinoviev, to replace the Second International, an international organisation of socialist parties. Comintern, or the Third International, aimed to co-ordinate the work of communist-style parties worldwide. However, instead of acting like an international body, Comintern aimed to subordinate all other communist parties to the direction of the Russian Communist Party.

The Russo-Polish War

The most controversial aspect of Lenin's policy was the Russo-Polish War of 1920/1. In April 1920, at the height of the Civil War,

Polish forces invaded the western Ukraine and occupied Kiev (Kyiv), but were later repulsed by the Red Army. According to David Marples, in *Lenin's Revolution: Russia, 1917–21* (2000), the Red Army led a counter-offensive that took them to the outskirts of Warsaw, the Polish capital. However, Lenin did not order a mere counter-offensive but rather a full-scale westward export of the revolution. In *The Unknown Lenin: From the Secret Archive (1996)*, Richard Pipes cites a political report of the Central Committee of the Russian Communist Party, produced on 20 September 1920, which makes clear that Lenin aimed to turn Poland into a communist state as a prelude to spreading revolution to the West. Indeed, Lenin was particularly hopeful that Britain would succumb to socialist revolution.

Lenin's hopes were wildly over-optimistic. The Red Army was defeated outside Warsaw in September 1920, and this forced a retreat. In April 1921 Soviet Russia signed the Treaty of Riga with Poland, which forced Russia to give up a large part of western Belorussia to the new Polish state. The prospect of spreading revolution westward had been an abject failure.

Lenin was more successful elsewhere, however. In 1917 the Mensheviks had established a democratic socialist government in Georgia and, in 1921 Lenin used the Georgian, Stalin, to overthrow it by force. By 1922 Georgia was incorporated into the new Soviet republic of Transcaucasia, which joined the USSR in December of that year.

Summary

By the time of his first stroke on 26 May 1922, Lenin had firmly established communist rule in Russia and had prevented the complete disintegration of the old Russian Empire. Although Finland, the Baltic States and Poland had achieved independence, the vast bulk of the old state was reconstituted as the USSR.

Lenin had also led the Bolsheviks/Communists to victory in the Civil War and, in the process, set up a dictatorship of the party with himself as undisputed leader. In achieving this end, political repression and terror had become an integral part of his regime.

Lenin's attempts to create a socialist economy and society were not so successful. Various attempts at socialism, including the 'commune state', state nationalisation and War Communism, only helped speed up Russia's economic collapse. The NEP of March 1921 was an admission of failure. Instead of creating a workers' state, Lenin had created a state of both workers and peasants.

By the time of his death, the socialist revolution was limited to the old Russian Empire. Attempts at exporting revolution had failed. It would take Lenin's successor, Stalin, and the might of the Red Army, to export socialism to Eastern Europe in 1944–8.

Q

Lenin: liberator or dictator? The Bolsheviks in power 1917–24

1. Read the following extract and then answer the question.

   '*The changes made by the Bolsheviks in their policies after the October Revolution were drastic. They had promised a popularly-elected government but disbanded the Constituent Assembly in January 1918 when they got less than a quarter of the seats.*

   '*They had promised the least repressive revolutionary regime in history. And yet, the Cheka, their security police, became unprecedentedly violent and arbitrary. They had promised economic reconstruction. Yet both the collapse of industry and the disruption of trade between town and countryside continued. And Lenin and his comrades had promised peace across Europe. They had assumed that their October Revolution would be followed, within weeks, if not days by revolutions against the European capitalist order. Instead they had signed the Treaty of Brest Litovsk in March 1918, giving up sovereignty over the Ukraine and the entire Baltic region.*'

   (adapted from Robert Service, *Lenin, A Political Life, Volume 3: The Iron Ring*, Palgrave Macmillan, 1994)

   Using the information in the extract above, and from this section, to what extent did Lenin fail to meet his aims in the years 1917 to 1924?

2. '*Lenin's greatest achievement after the October Revolution was to remain in power.*'

   How far do you agree with this view?

Lenin: an assessment

What was Lenin's contribution to the development of Russian socialism?

Lenin adapted Marx's ideas to fit Russian social and economic conditions and, faced with severe political repression under the Tsar, created a party model and structure that offered the opportunity for revolution, and which was later adopted by communist parties across the world.

However, Lenin's determination to be undisputed leader of Russian socialism caused the split of the RSDLP in 1903. His refusal to compromise with the Mensheviks or even members of his own Bolshevik faction proved divisive. As a result, Lenin succeeded in creating a Bolshevik dictatorship rather than a coalition socialist government. Lenin's character and the tactics he employed put an end to the hope of a democratic socialist Russia.

What part did Lenin play in the October Revolution?

Without the return of Lenin to Russia in 1917 there would have been no October Revolution. It was Lenin's determination to overthrow the Provisional Government that eventually led to the Bolshevik seizure of power. It was Lenin too who devised the programmes of 'Peace, Bread, Land', and 'All Power to the Soviets', which provided the Bolsheviks with popular support. However, unlike the February Revolution, the October Revolution was a planned seizure of power, using the Military Revolutionary Committee of the Petrograd Soviet as a front. Once in power, Lenin was determined not to give it up.

How successful was Lenin's rule in Russia?

Lenin overcame enormous odds to hold onto power until his death in 1924. Apart from a brief coalition with the Left SRs, the Bolsheviks ruled alone, fighting off political challengers and foreign intervention to win the Civil War.

However, Lenin was far less successful in trying to introduce socialism. The 'commune state', state nationalisation and War Communism all failed to create a strong socialist economy; his New Economic Policy (NEP) was a step back to a pre-socialist society.

Lenin created a centralised state controlled by the Communist Party in which terror and repression became an integral part of Bolshevik/Communist rule. Ultimately, Lenin went to his grave a partial failure. Despite his hopes that the October Revolution would be the beginning of a worldwide socialist revolution this was never to take place.

What was Lenin's legacy?

Mikhail Gorbachev, ruler of the USSR from 1985 to 1991, held up Lenin as an example of how to realistically develop socialism in Soviet Russia. This was in marked contrast to Lenin's successor, Stalin, who was portrayed as a repressive dictator. In reality Lenin had failed to bring about a social and economic revolution, but he had laid the foundations for Stalin's Soviet Union: a one-party dictatorship supported by state terror.

Further reading

Texts specifically designed for students

Acton, E. *Rethinking the Russian Revolution* (Hodder Arnold, 1990)

Laver, J. *Lenin: Liberator or Oppressor?* (Hodder Arnold, 1994)

Lee, S. J. *Lenin and Revolutionary Russia* (Routledge, 2003)

Morris, T. and Murphy, D. *Europe 1870–1991* (Collins, 2004)

Wood, A. *The Russian Revolution* (Longman, 1986)

Texts for more advanced study

Figes, O. *A People's Tragedy: The Russian Revolution 1891–1924* (Jonathan Cape, 1996) provides a detailed coverage of the era of the Russian Revolutions.

Pipes, R. *The Russian Revolution 1899–1919* (Harvill Press, 1990) offers a somewhat controversial view of the Russian Revolution.

Service, R. *Lenin: A Political Life – Volume 1: The Strength of Contradiction* (Palgrave Macmillan, 1985)

Service, R. *Lenin: A Political Life – Volume 2: Worlds in Collision* (Palgrave Macmillan, 1991)

Service R: *Lenin: A Political Life – Volume 3: The Iron Ring* (Palgrave Macmillan, 1994)
These three volumes give a very detailed insight into the political career of Lenin, with extensive use of Soviet and Russian archival material.

Volkogonov, D. *Lenin: Life and Legacy* (HarperCollins, 1994). A detailed study of the political career of Lenin and its impact on Soviet society.

Wade, R. *The Russian Revolution, 1917* (Cambridge University Press, 2000) offers a variety of historical explanations of the revolutionary year of 1917.

White, J.D. *Lenin: the Practice and Theory of Revolution* (Palgrave Macmillan, 2001) explains how Lenin's political ideas developed during the course of his life and how he was able to put many of them into practice after 1917.

Williams, B. *Lenin (Profiles in Power)* (Longman, 1999) provides an insight into the development of Lenin's ideas and his political career.

Index

Acknowledgements

The Publishers would like to thank the following for permission to reproduce extracts from their books:

Cambridge University Press for extracts from *The Russian Revolution, 1917* by Rex A. Wade (2000). Hodder Arnold for extracts from *Rethinking the Russia Revolution* by Edward Acton (1990) and from *Lenin and the Russian Revolution* (1970) by Christopher Hill. Palgrave Macmillan for extracts from *Lenin: A Political Life – Volume 3: The Iron Ring* (1994) by Robert Service. The Random House Group for extracts from *The Russian Revolution 1899–1919* by Richard Pipes (1990).

The Publishers would like to thank the following for permission to reproduce pictures on these pages T=Top, B=Bottom, L=Left, R=Right, C=Centre

akg-images, London 20; © Bettmann/Corbis 51B; © DACS 2004 *The Storming of the Winter Palace*, 1939 by Pavel Petrovich Sokolov-Skalja 38; © Getty Images/Hulton Archive 9, 11, 31B; David King Collection 10, 17, 26, 37, 39, 42, 38, 47, 51T, 56; Novosti (London) 12, 16, 18, 21, 24, 22, 31T, 36.

Cover picture: David King Collection

Every effort has been made to contact the holders of copyright material, but if any have been inadvertently overlooked the Publishers will be pleased to make the necessary arrangements at the first opportunity.